Rev. Booth,

May you continue to
serve the Lord in excelle[nce]
Don't grow weary in w[ell]

C. Lynn Busby
(Col. 3:17)

© 2015
Published in the United States by Nurturing Faith Inc., Macon GA,
www.nurturingfaith.net.

Library of Congress Cataloging-in-Publication Data is available.

ISBN 978-1-938514-60-9

*Unless otherwise indicated, scripture citations are taken from
the New Oxford Annotated Bible, New Revised Standard Version
(Oxford University Press, 2010).*

Dedicated to my daughter, Taylor,
who is my source of inspiration
and unconditional love

those who instruct them—and also to churches that will address critical elements of good preaching etiquette and offer practical ways to improve them.

This manual begins with an introduction on the history of etiquette and why it matters. Part one provides an exegetical analysis of key passages of scripture that deal with preaching etiquette. Part two suggests that if greater attention is given to matters of preaching etiquette, the ministry of preaching will be done decently and in order, and those charged with proclaiming God's word will be better equipped to serve in a spirit of excellence. Part three addresses matters of hospitality and honoraria viewed from studying 1 Corinthians 9:3-14, 3 John 5-8, and 1 Timothy 5:17-18. Following some personal reflection, I offer guidelines on conducting a seminar on preaching etiquette.

To assist the reader, an understanding of the following terms will be helpful:

Clergy:
A minister of the word in any capacity

Decorum:
A proper way to behave or exercise good manners

Etiquette:
The customary code of polite behavior under all circumstances of life

Honorarium:
A predetermined amount of money given to a preacher for ministry services

Love Offering:
A special offering collected during a worship service for a minister

Minister:
A title for a minister of the Word; one who preaches the gospel

Preaching:
A living interaction involving God, the preacher, and the congregation

Preaching Etiquette:
Appropriate conduct and manners related to the ministry of preaching

Protocol:
The formal and proper way of doing things in a decent and orderly fashion

Pulpit:
An elevated area in the sanctuary from which the preacher delivers the biblical message and where other ministers may be seated

Sacred Desk:
A pulpit stand or pulpit podium

Whooping (Whoop):
An African-American style of preaching that often occurs at the end of the sermon

In addition, the reader will note that throughout this study I use the words "pastor" and "preacher" interchangeably. Some preachers serve full time as pastor of a church and are often invited to preach in other settings as a guest. Other preachers may not serve as a pastor, but function as a shepherd through their preaching. This conversation on preaching etiquette applies to both full-time pastors and guest preachers. As Scott Gibson maintains, "Pastors are preachers and preachers are pastors."[3]

If ministers model appropriate pulpit decorum, preaching can be conducted in a more excellent way. Appropriate behavior in the pulpit includes but is not limited to pulpit attire, posture, and proclamation.

Notes

[1]H. Beecher Hicks Jr., *Preaching Through a Storm* (Grand Rapids: Zondervan, 1987), 104.

[2]L. Gregory Jones and Kevin R. Armstrong, *Resurrecting Excellence* (Grand Rapids: Eerdmans, 2006), 4.

[3]Scott Gibson, "Pastors and Preachers and Preachers and Pastors," podcast audio, https://itunes.apple.com/itunes-u/resources/Preaching.cfm-points-audio/id428971635 (accessed November 24, 2012).

Now you are the body of Christ and individually members of it. And God has appointed in the church first apostles, second prophets, third teachers; then deeds of power, then gifts of healing, forms of assistance, forms of leadership, various kinds of tongues. Are all apostles? Are all prophets? Are all teachers? Do all work miracles? Do all possess gifts of healing? Do all speak in tongues? Do all interpret? But strive for the greater gifts. And I will show you a still more excellent way.

—1 Corinthians 12:27-31

Or did the word of God originate with you? Or are you the only ones it has reached? Anyone who claims to be a prophet, or to have spiritual powers, must acknowledge that what I am writing to you is a command of the Lord. Anyone who does not recognize this is not to be recognized. So, my friends, be eager to prophesy, and do not forbid speaking in tongues; but all things should be done decently and in order.

—1 Corinthians 14:36-40

Beloved, you do faithfully whatever you do for the friends, even though they are strangers to you; they have testified to your love before the church. You will do well to send them on in a manner worthy of God; for they began their journey for the sake of Christ, accepting no support from non-believers. Therefore we ought to support such people, so that we may become co-workers with the truth.

—3 John 5-8

- Introduction -

Etiquette Matters

Each day we interact with people. We meet people of different races, genders, socioeconomic levels, cultural backgrounds, and upbringings. How we respond to one another on a daily basis can impact potential friendships, business partnerships, or ministry. Th bottom line is that etiquette matters, and over the years we have experienced shifts in what each generation deems to be proper behavior. Nevertheless, the goal in each society regarding rules of civility has always been to live together in harmony and mutual respect.

But what does etiquette have to do with preaching? After all, when we hear this word we often think of Emily Post, Amy Vanderbilt, or "Miss Manners"—women who may be the leading voices on protocol for propriety, but not protocol for preaching. Is it possible to welcome these women to a discussion on preaching etiquette?

In the ministry of preaching we tend to neglect attention to good manners both in and out of the pulpit. The goal of this book is to provide a manual on preaching etiquette that will provide tips on a more excellent way of leading worship and offering hospitality to preachers. This conversation will begin by answering the question about what is etiquette and how it relates to the proclamation of the Word.

The New Oxford American Dictionary defines etiquette as "the customary code of polite behavior in society or among members of a particular profession or group."[1] According to Naomi Torre, founding director of The Etiquette School, "Etiquette has to do with good manners. It's not so much our own good manners, but making other people feel comfortable by the way we behave."[2] Emily Post defined etiquette as "the technique of human conduct under all circumstances of life."[3] In an article in the *Dictionary of American History*, Diane Palmer gives highlights of the etiquette movement as summarized below.[4]

The history of civilized conduct can be traced to a book that an Egyptian government official wrote for his son in 2500 B.C. But the term "etiquette" did not come into use until the reign of Louis XIV (1638-1715) in France. Based on the French word "ticket," which denoted the proper paths for nobility to follow in the gardens of the palace of Versailles, etiquette rules provided a daily and precise list of functions related to times, places, and proper dress and behavior.

We learn many things from Paul's metaphor. First, we realize that every Christian is a necessary, beneficial member of the church. The church cannot function properly if it does not enlist the contributions of each of its members. This does not mean that we allow unqualified people to lead or teach because they think they are gifted in these areas . . . God calls us to be excited about spiritual gifts . . . he gives us gifts so we can build up the church, bear witness to the gospel, and honor and glorify him.[3]

A more excellent approach to preaching begins by recognizing that all believers have spiritual gifts to contribute to the worship experience. As it relates to the pulpit, pastors are the primary proclaimers in the church; however, pastors should avoid being territorial over the pulpit. Instead, we can offer hospitality to persons who feel called to preach by offering them opportunities to lead worship and/or Bible study and by assisting them with finding speaking opportunities outside the church. These common courtesies will help model the building, learning, and encouragement aspects of excellent worship that Paul advocated.

Speaking the Truth in Love

We also can demonstrate a more excellent way of leading from the pulpit by speaking the truth in love. Proverbs 25:11 provides tools for skillful living as it relates to the words we speak: "A word fitly spoken is like apples of gold in a setting of silver." A good sermon will proclaim the gospel in a spirit of love, compassion, and integrity. Paul extended this conversation by saying, "If I speak in the tongues of mortals and of angels, but do not have love, I am a noisy gong or a clanging cymbal. And if I have prophetic powers, and understand all mysteries and all knowledge, and if I have all faith, so as to remove mountains, but do not have love, I am nothing" (1 Cor. 13:1-3).

Clergy have a deep yearning to be loved or admired by people in the pews. We seek affirmation from those listening in hopes that the long hours spent in sermon preparation will pay off. However, good preaching etiquette does not seek praises from the congregants on whether a sermon is "good." As Gregory Jones and Kevin Armstrong state, "Excellence for Paul does not focus on what 'I' can do over against others, thereby creating 'winners' and 'losers.' Rather, Paul calls us—as he did the Corinthians—to a way of excelling by embodying God's love manifest in Jesus Christ."[4]

To serve God in excellence, speaking the truth of God's love manifest in Jesus Christ is prerequisite. Therefore, we must avoid calling names, venting church problems, or making personal pleas for a salary increase from the pulpit.

As Proverbs 15:23 reminds us, "To make an apt answer is a joy to anyone, and a word in season, how good it is!" Sermon delivery is also more than regurgitating exegetical work, offering self-help techniques, or giving illustrations that excite the crowd. These techniques may help complete the homiletical outline, but the end goal is far greater: giving God's word of encouragement and comfort. As Jeffrey D. Arthurs maintains, "We love and lead through our proclamation."[5] Proper decorum in the pulpit mirrors the love of Christ through both the message and the messenger.

Doing All Things Decently and in Order

Pulpit ministers are responsible for modeling appropriate conduct and ensuring that the worship service is conducted decently and in order. If they model orderliness in conduct and procedure, this aim can be achieved. But what does it mean to be "decent" and "in order"? Dennis Prutow, professor of homiletics and pastoral theology at Reformed Presbyterian Theological Seminary, offers this commentary on 1 Corinthians 14:21-40:

> The word translated "decently" is an adverb occurring only three times in the New Testament. It refers to acting respectably and doing things properly . . . The words translated "in order" refer to orderliness in conduct and procedure . . . The word "order" also appears five additional times in the book of Hebrews referring to the "order of Melchizedek" (Hebrews 5:6, 10; 6:20; 7:11, 17). A priestly order that involves set procedures followed assiduously . . . The "all things" of 1 Corinthians 14:40 therefore includes all those things pertaining to worship.[6]

Paul instructed the church at Corinth on proper decorum for exercising spiritual gifts in worship. There were obvious tensions he needed to address, and he wanted to be taken seriously. Paul informed the Corinthians that his words were a command from the Lord and not his own. Prutow captures the chaos that existed in the church:

> Corinth begins with a party spirit. . . . There also seems to have been an air of spiritual superiority among the members. . . . there was the grossest of sin, incest, permitted in the church. . . . these Christians were suing one another in civil court rather than attempting to settle their disputes civilly within the church. . . . There was confusion regarding the marital relationship . . . , eating meat sacrificed to idols, Christian liberty,

decorum in the pulpit by honoring God and one another in our differences. Roy Ciampa and Brian Rosner summarize this idea thus:

> Paul has already pointed out that "God is not a God of disorder" (14:33), and if everything (public worship above all!) is to be done for the glory of God (10:31), it should reflect his orderly nature . . . It is God's glory which is to be our preoccupation in worship, and that can be honored only when we maintain an atmosphere that does not distract people from his glory. Some Corinthians had manifested attitudes and behaviors which had drawn attention to themselves rather than to God, and which reflected a greater concern for self-edification than the edification of others.[14]

Our goal is not to foster an atmosphere where etiquette scorecards are kept on preachers, but to emphasize that etiquette matters and that those who lead from the pulpit should model appropriate behavior, maintain orderly worship, and minimize distractions. The messenger has to be mindful to promote Christ and not self. As Richard Pratt rightfully states, "Our worship must praise and honor God and build up and honor the church and its members. We should refrain from doing things in worship that do not edify the church, even if those things edify us personally. Our worship must be orderly."[15]

***

So how do we resurrect excellence in the pulpit? By building up the body of Christ, learning, and encouraging; by striving for the greater gifts, speaking the truth in love, and doing all things decently and in order so that we show others "a still more excellent way."

Notes

[1]H. Kelly Balmer, *Romans-1 Corinthians-2 Corinthians*, The Layman's Bible Commentary (Richmond: John Knox Press, 1970), 104-105.

[2]Robert Smith, Jr., *Doctrine That Dances* (Nashville: B&H Publishing Company, 2008), 22.

[3]Richard L. Pratt., *I & II Corinthians*, Holman New Testament Commentary, vol. 7 (Nashville: Holman Reference, 2000), 222.

[4]Gregory L. Jones and Kevin Armstrong, *Resurrecting Excellence: Shaping Faithful Christian Ministry* (Grand Rapids: Eerdmans, 2006), 1.

[5]Jeffrey D. Arthurs, "Give Them a Loaf, Not a Field," podcast audio, https://itunes.apple.com/itunes-u/resources/Preaching.cfm-points-audio/id428971635 (accessed November 25, 2012).

[6]Dennis Prutow, "Properly and Orderly." *Westminster Evangelistic Ministries*, 2005, http://www.wordfortheweek.org/learn/36 (accessed October 12, 2012).

- Part 2 -
Modeling Excellence in the Pulpit

Consider it improper to discuss etiquette without inviting Emily Post to the table. Post and the organization that followed her have been the leading voices on proper etiquette and decorum since the early 1900s. Although Post is deceased, her legacy continues through her heirs.

Nolan B. Harmon applies Emily Post's guidelines to ministers this way: "It has been our conviction that a minister, if a man, must be a gentleman; if a woman, a lady. This should almost go without saying. Thus we assume that a true Christian, man or woman, will instinctively know how to behave almost everywhere. This does not mean that the moment a minister is consecrated to God he or she will automatically know which fork to use first or understand all the vagaries of social protocol."[1]

As ministers of the gospel, we are called to preach and present ourselves well in the pulpit. But how do we do this? Haddon Robinson says we can't do better than Paul's counsel to Timothy: "Devote yourself to the public reading of Scripture, to preaching and to teaching. As you grow as a person, your sermons grow too. But it's also crucial to grow as a preacher. As people see you progress, they will respect you and respond to your ministry."[2] Robinson's classic book, *Biblical Preaching*, provides direction on how to improve pulpit etiquette: "The effectiveness of our sermons depends on two factors: what we say and how we say it."[3]

Roy E. De Brand provides further support for the need for good preaching etiquette, saying that "The first visual impression preachers make on a congregation is general appearance, including how we dress, the way we sit, how we stand, when it is time to preach, walking to the pulpit, and our posture in the pulpit."[4]

Therefore a review of the fundamental principles of etiquette, and their application to ministers (and congregations), is proper. These guidelines will both enhance pulpit ministry and ensure that all things are done decently and in order, which is an underlying goal. Although the tips offered here may seem basic, we should not assume ministers (or people in the pews) have been well-versed on matters of grooming and decorum.

- **Entering the Sanctuary:** Arrive prior to the time for which the service has been called. If this is not possible, avoid entering during prayers or announcements or the sermon.
- **Exiting the Sanctuary:** Avoid leaving during the sermon, prayers, communion, invitation, or benediction.
- **Guest Behavior**: Stand, kneel, read prayers aloud, and sing with those present unless these actions violate personal religious beliefs.
- **Holy Communion:** If communion is offered only to members of the local congregation, be reverent and avoid talking to others during this sacred time.
- **Technology:** Avoid taking pictures or making video or audio recordings without prior permission from the pastor.
- **Tithes and Offerings:** If you are a member of the local congregation, try to give at least ten percent of your gross salary. If you are a guest, between one and five dollars is appropriate, although optional.

Honesty

According to the Emily Post Institute, "Honesty ensures that we act sincerely and with integrity."[10] Jesus gave these same instructions when he preached the Sermon on the Mount. He admonished his followers to "let your word be 'Yes, Yes' or 'No, No'" (Matt. 5:37).

Here are a few tips from the Emily Post Institute that preachers can follow to model this principle: Check your calendar carefully. Once you've sent your response, you're committed. Changing a "yes" to a "no" is acceptable only if there is a good reason such as an illness or injury, a death in the family, or an unavoidable professional or business conflict. Post reminds us that "canceling because you have a 'better' offer is a surefire way to get dropped from everyone's guest lists."[11]

In addition to keeping our word, the principle of honesty also demands that we not plagiarize sermons. In his book *Should We Use Someone Else's Sermon?*, Scott Gibson argues that "the key is to be responsible with the gifts God has given us. We are to be faithful stewards. Plagiarism in preaching is the squandering of gifts that God gives to each preacher."[12] Haddon Robinson says, "If we take most of our material for a sermon from another preacher, then it is a matter of honesty and integrity that we give credit."[13] To avoid plagiarism, he suggests saying something like: "I came across an approach to a sermon by _____ and want to share it with you." Lillian Daniel adds the following comment to this conversation:

Giving Attention to Details

In addition to following the general principles of respect, consideration, and honesty—and where applicable, teaching these guidelines to their congregants—ministers must give strict attention to the specifics of proper decorum in the pulpit. Haddon Robinson, Kenneth Quick, Jeffrey Arthurs, Noland Harmon, and Roy De Brand offer the suggestions summarized below.[18]

Etiquette

- Be aware that mannerisms and repetitive behavior that may go unnoticed by friends and be tolerated by associates may scream for attention in the pulpit and thus divert listeners from what is said.
- Refrain from stuffing your hands in your pockets, stroking your hair or face, playing with a ring, fussing with a necktie or scarf, shuffling your feet, etc.
- Avoid using gestures that do not come naturally.
- Adhere to the time allotted for sermon delivery; avoid taking "time not granted."
- Refrain from using pauses/phrases such as "er," "and," "uh," "so," "ah," "you know," "like," "Amen," "Praise God," etc.
- Avoid using extra scriptures, stories, comments, etc. that communicate too little.

Dress

- Use grooming and dress techniques suited to the audience, situation, and speaker.
- As a general rule, dress one notch higher than the audience.
- Choose dark clothes over brightly colored ones.
- Ensure that clothing is neat, clean, well fitting, and coordinated.
- Keep dangling jewelry to a minimum.
- If female, wear a longer skirt.

Eye Contact

- Remember that eye contact probably ranks as the single most effective means of nonverbal communication; it helps to establish relationship.
- When speaking to a larger group, avoid fixed eye contact on individuals in favor of scanning a broad section of people.
- When speaking to a smaller group, look every person in the eye.

Movement

- Use disciplined body movement. Let your content motivate your actions.
- Identify annoying preaching mannerisms by recording yourself in audio and/or video and by using anonymous questionnaires to obtain honest feedback about

sermon length, content, and delivery. Then, focus on eliminating one annoying mannerism per month.

• Seek to overcome annoying pulpit mannerisms by moving from "unconscious incompetence" (you don't know what you are doing) to "conscience incompetence (you know you are doing it wrong) to "conscience competence" (you think about doing the right thing) to "unconscious competence" (you do the right thing and master mannerisms without thinking about it).[19]

Sitting/Standing

• Keep modesty and decorum in mind at all times.
• Sit or stand straight; never slouch.
• Keep socks pulled up and dresses pulled down over the knees.

Walking/Posture

• Take one or two deep breaths just before getting up to preach.
• Walk confidently (but not cockily) and at a normal pace to the pulpit.
• Stand straight but naturally and comfortably behind the pulpit.

Facial Expressions

• Maintain a pleasant, but not silly or inane, facial expression.
• While speaking, try to reflect in your face what you are saying.

Multimedia Enhancement

• Do not allow technological devices to hinder the message or increase sermon length or weaken delivery.
• Be sure devices are fully charged or plugged into a power outlet.
• Be mindful of "time-out" settings on devices that may occur during delivery.
• Ensure that audiovisual aids can be clearly seen/heard by people in the pews.

Pulpit Conduct

• Take care of personal needs such as smoothing your hair or arranging your clothes or accessories prior to entering the pulpit.
• Do not talk unnecessarily and/or laugh with a fellow minister in the pulpit.
• Avoid lounging in the chair or pulpit seat, moving about needlessly, or tending to trivial details.

Notes

[1]Nolan B. Harmon, *Ministerial Ethics and Etiquette* (Nashville: Abingdon Press, 1987), 11.

[2]Haddon Robinson, *Biblical Sermons: How Twelve Preachers Apply the Principles of Biblical Preaching* (Grand Rapids: Baker Book House, 1989), 30.

[3]Haddon Robinson, *Biblical Preaching* (Grand Rapids: Baker Books, 2001), 201.

[4]Roy De Brand, "The Visual in Preaching," in *The Handbook of Contemporary Preaching* (Nashville: Broadman Press, 1992), 398-407.

[5]Peggy Post, Anna Post, Lizzie Post, and Daniel Post Senning, *Emily Post's Etiquette: Manners for a New World,* 18th ed. (New York: HarperCollins, 2011), 5.

[6]Donald McCullough, *Say Please, Say Thank You: The Respect We Owe One Another* (New York: Perigee Books, 1998), 15.

[7]Post et al., *Etiquette,* 190.

[8]Post et al., *Etiquette,* 6.

[9]Arthur J. Magida, *How to Be a Perfect Stranger: A Guide to Etiquette in Other People's Religious Ceremonies* (Woodstock, VT: SkyLight Paths Publishing, 1996), 40-43.

[10]Post et al., *Etiquette,* 189-191.

[11]Post et al., *Etiquette,* 255-256.

[12]Scott M. Gibson, *Should We Use Someone Else's Sermon? Preaching in a Cut-and-Paste World* (Grand Rapids: Zondervan, 2008), 48

[13]Haddon Robinson, *The Art and Craft of Biblical Preaching: A Comprehensive Resource for Today's Communicators* (Grand Rapids: Zondervan, 2005), 586.

[14]Lillian Daniel and Martin B, Copenhaver *This Odd and Wondrous Calling: The Public and Private Lives of Two Ministers* (Grand Rapids: Eerdmans, 2009), 225.

[15]Robert Smith Jr., *Doctrine That Dances* (Nashville: B&H Publishing Group, 2008), 102.

[16]Louis W. Bloede, *The Effective Pastor: A Guide to Successful Ministry* (Minneapolis: Fortress Press, 1996), 153.

[17]Gardner C. Taylor and Edward L. Taylor, *The Words of Gardner Taylor* (Valley Forge: Judson Press, 2001), 284.

[18]Rf. Robinson, *Biblical Sermons*; Kenneth Quick, "Eliminating My Um, Um, Annoying Pulpit Mannerisms," in *The Art and Craft of Biblical Preaching*; Jeffrey Arthurs, "Master Annoying Mannerisms," podcast audio, https://itunes.apple.com/itunesu/resources/Preaching.cfm-points-audio/id428971635 (accessed November 22, 2012); Harmon, *Ministerial Ethics and Etiquette*; De Brand, "The Visual in Preaching."

[19]Arthurs, "Master Annoying Mannerisms.

[20]Alexander Strauch, *Biblical Eldership* (Littleton, CO: Lewis & Roth Publishers/Revised, 1995), 302-303.

[21]Jeffrey Arthurs and Scott Gibson, podcast audio, https://itunes.apple.com/itunesu/resources/Preaching.cfm-points-audio/id428971635 (accessed November 22, 2012).

[22]William H. Crouch Jr. and Joel C. Gregory, eds. *What We Love about the Black Church* (Valley Forge: Judson Press, 2010), 60.

[23]Daniel and Copenhaver. *This Odd and Wondrous Calling,* 79.

[24]Michael G. Cogdill, e-mail message to author, September 10, 2012.

[25]Dean Shriver, *Nobody's Perfect But You Have to Be* (Grand Rapids: Baker Books, 2005), 127.

Extending Hospitality in Biblical Times

The concept of providing hospitality dates back to biblical times. In Old Testament days, many Jews lived as nomads and relied upon others for food and shelter. In Genesis 18:2-5, Abraham models how to extend hospitality to guests:

> He looked up and saw three men standing near him. When he saw them, he ran from the tent entrance to meet them, and bowed down to the ground. He said, "My lord, if I find favor with you, do not pass by your servant. Let a little water be brought, and wash your feet, and rest yourselves under the tree. Let me bring a little bread, that you may refresh yourselves, and after that you may pass on—since you have come to your servant."

In New Testament days, many Christians experienced persecution and relied heavily on fellow Jews for support and encouragement. As Ralph Gower states, "It was particularly important for preachers of the time who had given up their livelihood so that they could preach the gospel. They were to be given hospitality for several days, and then encouraged to move on to another place. One could not be recognized as a leader in the church unless one was hospitable."[8]

Also, in New Testament days there were problems associated with those who traveled to proclaim the good news. It became a financial hardship for local congregations to provide lodging, protection, and other provisions. This is why the Apostle Paul spoke frequently about extending hospitality toward preachers.

Paul recognized the need for hospitality both for himself and his co-laborers. As a traveling missionary, he sought reasonable accommodations from Christians in Corinth. In Galatians 4:13-14, Paul said he was welcomed as if he were an angel of God. When Paul wrote to Philemon (1:22), he requested a guest room. And several times in the book of Romans, he requested hospitality (1:10, 15; 15:22-25, 28-29, 32).

Similarly, Paul did not forget Timothy: "If Timothy comes, see that he has nothing to fear among you, for he is doing the work of the Lord just as I am" (1 Cor. 16:10). Paul also appealed to the Romans to look out for Phoebe, a deacon in the church of Cenchreae: "Welcome her in the Lord as is fitting for the saints, and help her in whatever she may require from you, for she has been a benefactor of many and of myself as well" (Rom. 16:2).

Paul's plea for hospitality is evident in 1 Corinthians 9 where he asserts that traveling missionaries have the right not to work. As Andrew Arterbury puts it, "Paul reasons that the ones who sow spiritual seeds should be able to reap material benefits. Furthermore, Paul clarifies that Jesus was the one who instituted this policy."[9]

Even today, churches must consider if it is fiscally possible to host guest preachers. Likewise, guest ministers have to consider their travel, time away from home, appropriateness of the honorarium, and personal finances before accepting a preaching engagement.

Paul cited two scriptural precedents in his argument that a pastor/preacher should receive an honorable wage or fee. The first comes from the law: do not muzzle an ox (Deut. 25:4). The second points to Jesus' teaching: the worker deserves his wages (Luke 10:7).

Oxen were used in biblical times and also today in some underdeveloped countries in the threshing of grain. In this process, a pair of oxen is yoked together and then the yoke is attached to a vertical pole set in the middle of the threshing floor. Led by a young farmer, the oxen move around the threshing floor as their hooves do all the work. The Bible describes this process as a strenuous task so the oxen should not be muzzled, thus preventing them from eating. It would be harsh treatment to hinder an ox that is working hard to provide food for the community.[10]

Paul applied this analogy to those who preach the gospel. Preachers should not be hindered from their work—preaching the gospel—and their labor should be supported in wages. As Thomas Oden writes, "It is only right that they receive at least minimal, fair, decent maintenance."[11]

The authors of Eerdmans' *Pulpit Commentary* on Corinthians suggest a minister's right to claim adequate support is enforced by this analogy: "The soldier in service to his country receives maintenance; the planter in the vineyard eats of its fruit; the shepherd finds the means of his support in the flock which he tends. Therefore, the Christian minister is a solder, fighting the battles of the Lord and of his Church; a labourer in the vineyard of Christ . . . a shepherd, watching over the sheep."[12]

George T. Montague's interpretation on preachers and compensation also expresses the early church focus on ministerial excellence:

> The word honor can also have the meaning "wage, stipend, salary." Both meanings seem to rule here. Are the presbyters occupied full time at their ministry? We can't be sure, but it is obvious they are not mere volunteers. The early Church realized that these ministries were important enough to endow them with monetary support and to encourage excellence by rewarding with additional stipend—double—those who do their service well. This would be especially true of those who preach and teach.[13]

Parking

- Reserve a parking space near the entrance of the church for the guest and notify the person of its location.
- Ask for the make and model of the vehicle the guest will be driving.
- Greet the guest at the parking space and escort him or her into the building.

Assistance

- Be aware of the time the guest will arrive at the church.
- Know whether the guest will be traveling alone or with a spouse or assistant. If the latter, determine seating arrangements for that person before the arrival.
- Arrange for someone to assist the guest and travel companion.
- Be prepared to assist any guest who may have a special physical need.

Meals

- Ask the guest about drink preferences before, during, and after speaking.
- Inquire about food allergies and/or preferences.
- Before an early worship service, have a fruit tray, juice, and coffee available.
- If the church has multiple worship services, consider serving breakfast.

Providing Honoraria to Guest Ministers

In addition to receiving hospitable treatment prior to and during their visits, guest ministers should receive a respectable honorarium. I have heard critics say that ministers are doing God's work and should not be paid, but persons who feel this way have no idea the amount of time and energy spent in preparation for a speaking engagement.

Paul stated the case for payment in 1 Corinthians 9:3-14, and Richard L. Pratt Jr. supports his argument with these words: "Paul led up to the question of why he and Barnabas did not take advantage of what they had rights to enjoy. . . . He appealed not only to the example of the other church leaders but also to common daily life. Common sense dictates that people have a right to make a living from their work. Paul insisted that God agreed to these rights, and the Scripture proved the point."[17]

Do not be alarmed if a guest minister sends a contract to your church after an invitation has been extended. The first time my church received such a contract, I was appalled. But as I started receiving more frequent preaching invitations myself, I quickly grew to understand the need for a contract. Often, hospitality toward guest ministers is not extended appropriately. As a result, they must use personal funds to travel to the speaking engagement. Therefore, establishing the honorarium in writing beforehand is a significant aspect of hospitality.

In a conversation I had once with Haddon Robinson, he shared a personal experience about an out-of-town speaking engagement. Robinson purchased his plane ticket, traveled out of state, and covered his meal expenses. When he returned home from this engagement, he opened the envelope from the church and discovered a $50 honorarium. To his chagrin, Robinson deemed it necessary to use this as a teaching moment. He returned the check and enclosed a personal letter. In the letter he asked the church to keep the check but to reconsider how it offers hospitality to guest ministers in the future. As one might expect, Robinson never heard from that church again.[18]

Some churches may be opposed to dealing in contracts when it comes to preaching. If so, expectations on both ends should be made crystal clear in advance. The honorarium should be communicated up front when the invitation is extended. Good hospitality dictates that the host church should provide airfare, hotel, and meals for all invited out-of-town speakers.

It is also helpful to note J. Daniel Day's position on this topic. Day, a longtime pastor and church leader, encourages churches to write separate checks for the honorarium and travel, saying:

> Churches can eliminate an unnecessary accounting hassle for guest ministers either 1) by writing one check to reimburse traveling expenses (mileage, meals enroute, etc.) and another check for the honorarium, or 2) by writing on the memo line of the one check given to the guest minister the amount that is understood by the church as reimbursement for traveling expenses and the amount that is understood as honorarium. Unless this division is designated by the church, the guest minister, in reporting her income for tax purposes, must preserve records for expenses incurred to earn that income and then complete a separate tax form to deduct her "business expenses." If, however, the host church has thoughtfully indicated that division on one check (or issued two separate checks), the minister is relieved of an accounting burden that really should be the church's. Another obvious gain in this practice is

that it trains churches to recognize that a $200 honorarium (when the preacher must pay his or her traveling expenses) often means the actual income the preacher "earns" is substantially less than the face amount of the honorarium check.[19]

Prior to a speaker's arrival, the host church should prepare the check as indicated above. (Suggestions for honorarium amounts are found on page 43.) If a church will pay the speaker $600 or more in a given year, a W-9 form should accompany the honorarium check(s). Minor changes to this process or the check amounts may be needed if a "love offering" is given directly to the guest preacher. Such offerings must be reported as taxable income on a Form 1099-MISC if $600 or more.[20]

In the final analysis, good preaching etiquette is considerate of guest ministers. They have financial obligations just like those persons who listen to their sermons. Host churches should offer exceptional hospitality and ensure that guest preachers receive at the least a fair honorarium.

Weddings and Funerals

In addition to preaching honorariums, it is proper etiquette to provide an honorarium plus travel expenses to ministers who officiate weddings and funerals.

Chris McDaniel, chief business development officer of DELTA Ministries International and author of *Igniting a Life of Generosity*, offers the following pay scale as a guide for determining a wedding honorarium. The amounts differ based on the circumstances and on whether or not the people being married are members of the church.[21]

$100 – small with a rehearsal but no premarital counseling
$150 – some advance preparation but no premarital counseling
$300 – advance preparation and premarital counseling
More than $300 – A generous gift

When considering McDaniel's suggested pay scale, one must ask if it is fair, gracious, or generous. One might argue that it is certainly not generous. In fact, considering the amount of time and preparation weddings require of ministers, then McDaniel's pay scale may seem unfair. Most people I have consulted agree with McDaniel, noting that ministers should receive between $100-200 to conduct weddings requiring little time and preparation.

***

Pulpit hospitality is vastly different from true Christian hospitality. Christian hospitality is uncomfortable, welcomes the stranger, and involves risks. Jesus certainly spent a large part of his ministry taking risks and welcoming vulnerable groups such as the poor, sick, and orphaned. With that said, I understand how this conversation about the hospitality needs of ministers might make some feel uncomfortable. Nevertheless, the "elephant in the room" needs to be addressed.

Hospitality and proper behavior are key components of resurrecting excellence in the ministry of preaching, and the church has failed to offer guidelines on how to do it successfully. As previously mentioned, the first and most important rule of good manners is kindness, respect, and consideration toward others. As a matter of fact, the second most important commandment next to loving God is this: "You shall love your neighbor as yourself" (Matt. 22:39). Good preaching etiquette will extend the best possible hospitality to those both in and out of the pulpit.

Notes

[1]William H. Willimon, *Pastor: The Theology and Practice of Ordained Ministry* (Nashville: Abingdon Press, 2002), 164.

[2]Christine D. Pohl, *Making Room: Recovering Hospitality as a Christian Tradition* (Grand Rapids: Eerdmans, 1999), 31.

[3]Haddon Robinson, "A Congress on Hospitality," (devotional, June 2, 2006) http://odb. org/2006/06/02/a-congress-on-hospitality/ (accessed June 12, 2013).

[4]Haddon Robinson, "Shake Hands Before You Preach," podcast audio, https://itunes.apple. com/itunesu/resources/Preaching.cfm-points-audio/id428971635 (accessed November 24, 2012).

[5]Lillian Daniel and Martin B. Copenhaver, *This Odd and Wondrous Calling* (Grand Rapids: Eerdmans, 2009), 11-15.

[6]Peggy Post, Anna Post, Lizzie Post, and Daniel Post Senning, *Emily Post's Etiquette: Manners for a New World,* 18th ed. (New York: HarperCollins, 2011), 6.

[7]Leslie B. Flynn, *Did I Say Thanks?* (Nashville: Broadman Press, 1963), 24.

[8]Ralph Gower, *The New Manners and Customs of Bible Times* (Chicago: Moody Press,1987), 241-242.

[9]Andrew Arterbury, *Entertaining Angels: Early Christian Hospitality in its Mediterranean Setting* (Sheffield, UK: Sheffield Phoenix Press, 2005), 98.

[10]George T. Montague, *First and Second Timothy, Titus* (Grand Rapids: Baker Academic Books, 2008), 113. Gower, *New Manners and Customs,* 97.

[11]Thomas C. Oden, *First and Second Timothy and Titus,* Interpretation (Louisville, KY: John Knox Press, 1989), 151.

[12]E. Hurndall, C. Lipscomb, D. Fraser, J. R. Thompson, R. Tuck, J. Waite, and H. Bremner, "Corinthians," in the *Pulpit Commentary,* vol. 19 (Grand Rapids: Eerdmans, 1977), 303.

[13]Montague, *First and Second Timothy,* 113.

[14]Knute Larson, *First and Second Thessalonians, First and Second Timothy, Titus, Philemon* (Nashville: Broadman and Holman Publishers, 2000), 226.

- Conclusion -
A More Excellent Way

As I conclude this study, I want to further support the importance of preaching etiquette by telling about one of my preaching engagements. This experience speaks volumes to what I have presented in this book and also voices the tensions associated with this subject.

Using the sermon title "Guess Who's Coming to Dinner," I shared with the congregation from Luke 17:5-10. The sermon dealt with the "big idea" regarding faith, and concluded with emphasis on verse 10: "So you also, when you have done all that you were ordered to do, say, 'We are worthless slaves; we have done only what we ought to have done!'" This scripture simply means that, according to Leander Keck, "Even when the servant has done all that is required of him, he is still 'worthless' or 'unworthy.' Our inclination is to think that if we do what we are commanded, we deserve some reward. . . . God owes us nothing for living good Christian lives. God's favor and blessing are matters of grace—they cannot be earned."[1] Little did I know this text would soon become a reality.

After the sermon was over I went back to the pastor's office. We exchanged pleasantries regarding the worship service, and then the pastor handed me a W-9 form. I praised him for following "good preaching etiquette." I shared some of my research on this subject, and then the pastor said, "Oh my. Please don't tell anyone that I forgot to do this beforehand." To my chagrin, the church did not have a check ready to present to me following the service. I had just spent the night in a hotel, traveled a total of 140 miles, paid for my meals, and was hoping for some reimbursement. As a single parent, this trip was a hit to my budget. After more than a year, at the writing of this chapter, I have yet to receive an honorarium from the church.

So here lies the tension I have with my pursuit for resurrecting excellence in the pulpit. On the one hand I affirm that proper decorum in the pulpit is important. Preachers should model appropriate dress, manners, and communication skills. I also affirm that host churches should offer the best hospitality possible toward guest ministers. This includes the consideration of travel arrangements, accommodations, meals, and certainly an honorarium. Yet, after preaching this sermon from Luke 17:5-10, I was forced to ask myself: "Do you practice what you preach?" How do I make sense of Luke 17:10 and 1 Corinthians 9:3-14? Is it

Sample Hospitality Form

(Speaker's name)
(Speaker's address)

Dear (Speaker),

Thank you for accepting our invitation to preach on (Date) at (name of church or chapel). Our worship service typically lasts (amount of time). Guest ministers have (amount of time) to deliver the message. Here is some information that may assist you as you prepare to worship with us:

Honorarium:
Church address:
Church phone:
Service date:
Service time:
Host pastor/person:
Host's email:
Host's cell phone:

(The host will be at the church 30 minutes before the start of the service to greet you.)

Hotel information:

Please communicate the following information to the host person listed above:
Sermon title by (Date)
Suggested hymns, readings
Short biography of yourself
Name(s) of guest(s) who will accompany you
Special needs (ex: physical, dietary)

If you have any questions, please contact your host or the church office.

CC: Host

Enclosures:
Map of church
Sample order of service

Suggested Preaching Honoraria

The following amounts come from feedback I received from focus groups and Doctor of Ministry (D.Min.) co-hort surveys. These are offered only as suggestions and should not negate a seasoned, highly respected, and established preacher from being considered in the higher honorarium ranges due to the lack of a seminary education.

$100	preparation
$200	preparation + 3-5 years ministry experience
$200-$250	preparation + experience + master's degree (ex: M.Div.)
$250-$300	preparation + doctoral degree (ex: D.Min., Ph.D.)
$300-$350	preparation + esteemed ministry position (ex: professor, well-known preacher, author)

*Write separate checks for the honorarium and travel expenses (ex: mileage reimbursement at the current IRS rate, meals, hotel). Or, write one check and in the memo line specify the amount for each (ex: $300 honorarium / $200 travel). Be sure to present the honorarium to the speaker/officiant as soon as the ministry services have been rendered.

Teaching Notes

Begin with a brief introduction of yourself and why you feel preaching etiquette is an important subject. Welcome participants and thank them for attending. Depending on the size of the group and the time available, it may be helpful to ask participants about their current ministry role and what attracted them to attend a seminar on this subject.

Purpose

The purpose of this seminar is to increase awareness about matters of preaching etiquette to help ensure that all things are done "decently and in order," as 1 Corinthians 14:40 tells us. I must preface this statement by making it clear that what is considered decently and in order will be different depending on the ministerial context. I intend to offer general guidelines and obtain participant feedback on ways churches might resurrect excellence in the pulpit and the preacher.

Goals

My goals in this seminar are to:
- **Increase Awareness (A):** Before you leave today, I hope you will have a greater understanding of biblical passages that address preaching etiquette—particularly as they relate to proper decorum, hospitality, and compensation.
- **Increase Conversation (C):** Perhaps something will be said in this seminar that might inspire you to start a conversation in your church about some of the topics we will cover.
- **Increase Training (T):** We have a responsibility to prepare ourselves and to equip future leaders to serve God in a spirit of excellence. This seminar will provide necessary tools to help you train others on matters of etiquette.
- So the overarching goal is for you to **ACT**! Take this information back to your local church, start a conversation that has been avoided or neglected, and allow the information provided to resurrect excellence in the preaching ministry.

Note of Clarification/Explanation

Throughout this seminar I will use the words "pastor and preacher" interchangeably. There are preachers who serve full time as a pastor of a church and are often invited to preach in other settings as a guest. There are also preachers who may not serve as pastor of a church but function as a shepherd

Questionnaire on Preaching Etiquette

*Please provide your birth month and day for identification purposes and to maintain anonymity. _____

Confidentiality Statement

Records of participation in this research project will be kept confidential to the extent permitted by law. This questionnaire is designed to explore matters of preaching etiquette. The information you provide will be helpful for creating a manual on preaching etiquette to be used in the local church. This study is being conducted by C. Lynn Brinkley, Doctorate of Ministry student, Gordon-Conwell Theological Seminary. Please be assured that all of your answers will be kept strictly confidential. The information you provide will be presented only in summary form, in combination with the responses of other participants in this study. The answers you give will never be linked with your name. By completing this questionnaire, you have given your consent to be a voluntary participant in this study.

Demographics

1. What is your age?
o 18 to 24
o 25 to 34
o 35 to 44
o 45 to 54
o 55 to 64
o 65 to 74
o 75 or older

2. What is the highest degree or level of school you have completed? If currently enrolled, the highest degree received.
o No schooling completed
o Nursery school to 8th grade
o Some high school, no diploma

o High school graduate, diploma or the equivalent (e.g.: GED)

o Some college credit, no degree

o Trade/technical/vocational training

o Associate's degree

o Bachelor's degree

o Master's degree

o Professional degree

o Doctorate degree

3. What is your gender?

o Female

o Male

4. What is your race/ethnic background?

o African American/Black

o Asian /Pacific Islander

o Caucasian/White

o Hispanic or Latino

o Native American or American Indian

o Mixed ethnicity

o Other, please specify_____

5. What is your religious denomination?

6. Please write your assigned ID number below.

Preaching Etiquette

7. What is your level of interest in learning about pulpit mannerisms and ways to offer hospitality to guest ministers?

o I have a very high level of interest.

o I have a somewhat high level of interest.

o I have a moderate level of interest.

o I have a somewhat low level of interest.

o I have a very low level of interest.

o I have no interest.

18. The Bible teaches that ministers should receive financial support for their labor.
o Strongly Disagree
o Disagree
o Neither Agree nor Disagree
o Agree
o Strongly Agree

19. The Bible teaches that hospitality should be offered to traveling ministers/missionaries.
o Strongly Disagree
o Disagree
o Neither Agree nor Disagree
o Agree
o Strongly Agree

20. I think persons in the pews should keep silent during sermon delivery and not make verbal responses to the message.
o Strongly Disagree
o Disagree
o Neither Agree nor Disagree
o Agree
o Strongly Agree

21. I think pastors/ministers should be addressed by church members as "Pastor," or "Reverend," or "Reverend Doctor" instead of their first names.
o Strongly Disagree
o Disagree
o Neither Agree nor Disagree
o Agree
o Strongly Agree

CPSIA information can be obtained at www.ICGtesting.com
Printed in the USA
BVOW11s0834260116

434243BV00001B/4/P